TURNER IN THE CLORE GALLERY

TURNER

in the Clore Gallery

An Illustrated Guide

THE TATE GALLERY

cover
The Bay of Baiae, with Apollo and the Sibyl 1823 (detail)

frontispiece
Self-portrait c.1799

ISBN 1 85437 101 0 (paper)
First published by order of the Trustees 1987
Second edition 1987
Third, revised, edition 1992
Fourth, revised, edition 1994
This book was originally published as
The Turner Collection in the Clore Gallery
Copyright © Tate Gallery 1987 All rights reserved
Designed and published by Tate Gallery Publications,
Millbank, London SW1P 4RG
Photographic credits: John Webb FRPS
Tate Gallery Photographic Department
Printed in Great Britain by Balding + Mansell,
Peterborough, Cambridgeshire

Contents

J.M.W. Turner

Joseph Mallord William Turner was born in 1775, and died in 1851. His lifespan embraced what was perhaps the most fruitful of all periods in British art – an age that began with the achievements of Hogarth, Reynolds, Gainsborough and Wilson, continued into the epoch of high Romanticism, of Blake, Lawrence, Constable and Bonington, and concluded amid the novelties of Pre-Raphaelitism and Victorian realism. Turner himself seems in retrospect to preside over the whole period as the greatest figure of a host of great men, the culmination, almost the definition, of the Romantic artist. He grew up when the Royal Academy was newly founded and the British school still rather self-consciously unsure of its credentials; his death coincided almost exactly with the date prophesied by John Constable when in 1822 he wrote: 'The art will go out: there will be no genuine painting in England in thirty years.'

Turner's Gallery

Turner was a professional artist from his earliest youth. He first began to exhibit his work publicly when he was still a boy, hanging watercolours in the window of his father's barber-shop in Maiden Lane, Covent Garden, and selling them for a few shillings each. At the age of fifteen, in 1790, he sent one of his views to the Royal Academy, where it was shown in the summer exhibition that year. Thereafter, for the rest of his life, he regularly submitted paintings and watercolours to the Academy. But the desire to keep his work before the public was not satisfied by this. In 1799, the year in which he was elected an Associate of the Academy, he took rooms in a house in Harley Street where, by 1804, he had built himself a gallery in which he could display twenty or thirty pictures. Here, for a number of years, he held his own annual exhibitions. In 1810 he moved to a house close by, at 47 Queen Anne Street West: to this, too, he added a gallery, which was finished in 1821 to his own careful designs and hung with dark red paper. But whereas in his early days he had announced regular exhibitions and encouraged the public to view, while prohibiting sketching from his exhibits, in his later life he was reclusive and jealous of his privacy. It became a matter of fascination among art-lovers to contrive access to Turner's Gallery, and there is a fund of anecdote and reminiscence describing the eccentric conditions in which the artist lived:

> The door was opened by a woman, for whom one hardly knew what to feel most, terror or pity … She showed us into a dining-room, which had penury and meanness written on every wall and article of furniture. Then up into the gallery; a fine room – indeed, one of the best in London, but in a dilapidated state; his pictures the same. The great 'Risc of Carthage' all mildewed and flaking off; … he uncovered a few matchless creatures, fresh and dewy, like pearls just set – the mere colours grateful to the eye without reference to the subjects … The old gentleman was great fun …

After the death of his father in 1829 Turner made his first will. He was fifty-four years old and at the height of his career, but the personal tragedy made him newly conscious of the uncertainty of life and the need to make explicit his complicated plans. He bequeathed two of the most celebrated of his earlier masterpieces to the National Gallery, on condition that they should always hang between two paintings by his great French predecessor Claude Lorraine. The pictures in question, 'Dido building Carthage' and 'The Decline of Carthage', were both works that owed much to the seventeenth-century master. They announced, in fact, that Turner's lifelong ambition to emulate and surpass Claude had, in his own estimation, been realised. It was a gesture of triumph.

He never changed the terms of this unusual bequest to the National Gallery, although he had at one point, perhaps jokingly, expressed the wish to be buried in the canvas of 'Dido building Carthage'. But in a new will of 1831 he changed the second of the two pictures to 'Sun rising through vapour'. He soon had further thoughts about the rest of his large output. His fellow Academician the architect Sir John Soane was in the process of having a Bill passed by Parliament to permit him to leave his house in Lincoln's Inn Fields to the public as a museum. The idea obviously attracted Turner, who in August 1832 drafted a strange, muddled codicil to his will in which he directed that funds were to be made available from his estate 'for the erection of the Gallery to hold my Pictures' and for the accommodation of one or more custodians. This was to be done 'keeping in view the first objects I direct namely is to keep my pictures together so that they may be seen known or found at the discretion'. He continued: 'as to the mode how they may be viewed gratuitously I leave to my Executors'. The wording is unclear but it seems that Turner intended this new gallery to form part of a 'Charitable Institution for the Maintenance and Support of Male Decayed Artists' for which he had provided in his original will. If this Charity were not instituted, he directed his Executors ' to keep all the Pictures and Property in Queen Ann St West No 47 intire and unsold' and to maintain them there as 'Turner's Gallery'. He appointed his long-standing housekeeper Hannah Danby as 'Custodian and Keeper of the Pictures Houses and Premises', while the Executors were 'to keep the said Gallery in a viewable state at all times concurring with the object of keeping my works together and to be seen under certain restrictions which may be most reputable and advisable'. This odd document was never attested, and is, at best, only a vague fore-shadowing of ideas that were to crystalise in his mind much later. They received an important catalyst in 1847, when the collector Robert Vernon gave a large group of modern British pictures to the National Gallery, among them four by Turner. Although lack of space prevented the Trustees displaying Vernon's collection, they did hang one work – Turner's Venetian view of 'The Dogano, San Giorgio, Citella, from the steps of the Europa'. These developments seem to have provided the clarification needed for his own intentions, and on 2 August 1848 he added a new, and properly draft-ed, codicil to his will. This specified that the works with which he was con-cerned were his 'finished pictures' – about 100 of these were counted in his studio after his death. It was this group that he insisted must be 'kept togeth-er'. 'Sun rising through vapour' and 'Dido building Carthage' were to go to the National Gallery as originally planned; but now all the finished pictures were also 'bequeathed unto the Trustees of the National Gallery provided that a room or rooms are added to the present National Gallery to be when erected called "Turner's Gallery" in which such pictures are to be constant-ly kept deposited and preserved'. If these conditions were not met the pic-tures were to remain at Queen Anne Street, under the guardianship of Hannah Danby (or a successor to be appointed by the Trustees) until the lease of the property could no longer be renewed; then they were to be sold. Turner made no mention of the remaining contents of his studio and gallery – some 180 oil sketches and over 19,000 drawings, many in sketch books, so it may be assumed that these were intended to be sold as part of the estate. As an afterthought he added to this codicil the proviso that, following the expiry of the Queen Anne Street lease, the National Gallery might have five years to construct the new 'Turner Gallery', or forfeit the pictures. A further codicil of 1 February 1849 modified this slightly, declaring the gift void if the Trustees of the National Gallery had not provided accommodation for the pictures ten years after Turner's death. The proceeds from the sale of the pictures were to be divided between the Royal Academy Pension Fund, the Artist's General Benevolent Fund and, of course, his own Institution for Decayed Artists.

He died on 19 December 1851 at the age of 76. He was buried according sketchbooks from the Bequest, with prints and pictures lent from collections throughout the world. The exhibition prompted a new urge to see the range of his output under one roof, and – although he had never explicitly given so many of his works to the Nation – it was felt that the only way in which full justice could be done to his many-sided genius was for a new gallery to be found in which provision was made for the display of all aspects of his art. In 1980 a magnificent offer by the Clore Foundation made it possible for the Trustees of the Tate Gallery to commission a new wing of the building for that purpose. A further generous donation from the Foundation provided for a substantial refurbishment of the Clore Gallery in 1994.

Bibliographical Note

The oil paintings in the Turner Bequest are listed in the Tate Gallery's *Concise Catalogue*, and, with comprehensive descriptions, in the standard *catalogue raisonné* of Turner's works, by Martin Butlin and Evelyn Joll, *The Paintings of J.M.W. Turner*, 2 vols. (revised edition, London, 1984). The works on paper are described in A.J. Finberg's *Inventory of the Drawings; in the Turner Bequest* (1909). Detailed, revised catalogues are in preparation.

The Clore Gallery from
the Tate Gallery Steps

Room T1 looking
towards Rooms T5 and T9

The Main Entrance from the
Garden Terrace

The Clore Gallery

The Clore Gallery, designed by James Stirling, Michael Wilford and Associates, shows Turner's work in a suite of nine principal galleries. A further gallery on the floor above provides space for the hanging of the remainder of the oil paintings as a study collection. There are also two galleries on the upper level for exhibitions and watercolours. The collection comprises almost three-fifths of Turner's considerable output in oil. As he wished, the display of pictures in the principal galleries is changed from time to time, especially when pictures are sent for exhibition elsewhere.

In addition to the paintings, the Gallery holds some 280 sketchbooks and about 10,000 watercolours and drawings. Temporary exhibitions, most often of works on paper and usually changing three times a year, are held in two rooms on the second floor. Works on paper not on show, including a representative collection of prints after Turner's designs, can be examined by appointment in the Study Room, also on the second floor. Visitors have access to related photographic collections, a microfilm reader and a library of reference material. The Tate Gallery's collection of British drawings and watercolours by artists born before 1880 may also be studied here. Thus the Clore Gallery provides a comprehensive survey of the whole of Turner's output in its context, from his earliest surviving sketches to his latest exhibited masterpieces; the complete range of his sketchbooks (only four are known to be in collections elsewhere) and thousands of colour studies, in both oil and watercolour, give an exceptionally complete insight into his creative processes. A display of personal relics and documents, in gallery 000, adds a further, biographical dimension to the representation of the man as well as the artist. This and other areas of the collections will from time to time be augmented by loans.

High Art, History and the Sublime

Turner had been practising as a watercolourist for nearly a decade when he sent his first oil painting to the Royal Academy's spring exhibition in 1796. In both medium and subject-matter 'Fishermen at Sea' marked a new departure: the heaving surface of the sea and effect of moonlight were themes that he had experimented with in earlier drawings but never rendered with such consummate polish. It is a canvas that throws down the gauntlet to the most accomplished landscape and marine painters of the day, and proclaims its superiority to them all. The exhibited pictures of the next few years, before and after his election first as Associate (1799) and then as full Member (1802) of the Academy, continued to be ambitious in conception and, increasingly, in scale as well. The first of the principal galleries presents his work of this period, and shows him deliberately aiming to over-awe his audience according to the demands of the 'Grand Style'. The eighteenth-century theory of the Sublime held that serious art should deal with the noblest and most powerful themes and Turner set out to show that landscape could meet these high expectations. He began with landscape subjects of a picuresquely dramatic order, drawing on his travels in the north of England: 'Buttermere Lake, with Part of Cromackwater, Cumberland, a Shower' is one of the finest of these, with its assured evocation of the scale of the Lakeland hills and their grand, if fleeting, climatic effects. But many of the most significant stages of his development at this period were marked by ambitious marines. In 1803 Turner exhibited 'Calais Pier' (National Gallery), painted just after he had been elected Royal Academician. This reflects the influence of the sea-pieces of Ruysdael that he had seen during his visit to Paris in 1802, but also arose from a personal experience, his landing at Calais. It is the first of a long and important sequence of pictures, produced at different times in the artist's life, which are inspired by the incidents of his tireless travelling. A still more vividly immediate rendering of the violence of the sea followed in the celebrated 'Shipwreck' which Turner showed in 1805, where his concern with the plight of human beings at the mercy of nature is revealed in carefully individualised figures and lively characterisation.

In a more generalised and still grander idiom, he went on to produce scenes illustrating cataclysms from Biblical or ancient history. Three of these dominate the room: 'The Destruction of Sodom', possible shown at Turn-

Fisherman at Sea
1796 (detail)

ers's own gallery in 1805, but apparently left unfinished; 'The Deluge' of about the same date, and 'Snow Storm: Hannibal and his Army Crossing the Alps' which appeared at the Academy in 1812. Less turbulent though equally disturbing in its way is 'Apollo and Python', shown in 1811, which displays in allegorical guise the struggle of light and darkness, good and evil.

To many of these pictures Turner appended appropriate quotations from Milton, Thomson and other literary sources, amplifying the ideas propounded in the compositions themselves. In the case of 'Hannibal', the verses he published were of his own making, and were attributed to a 'Manuscript Poem, Fallacies of Hope'. The 'Fallacies of Hope' was to alternate with Thomson and Byron in Turner's catalogue entries for the remainder of his life, but it seems never to have reached a final or definitive form; indeed, it is rather a collective title for a group of fragments written to explicate the pictures than a coherent work in its own right. The artist's notebooks of the first decade of the century are full of jottings towards poems which rarely achieved completion and, despite the evident seriousness with which Turner regarded these essays, it has to be admitted that they betray no great literary talent.

The allusions to more enduring works of literature are wide-ranging. Milton was the modern British equivalent of Homer and Virgil, and Turner evoked his *Paradise Lost* as well as the Bible when he painted the dark, swirling 'Deluge' with its heroic, large-scale figures. An even more recent poet who engrossed his interest later was Byron: the first time Byron's work was quoted by Turner was in connection with his highly-charged nocturne 'The Field of Waterloo', shown at the Academy in 1818. This intensely romantic meditation on the suffering and loss occasioned by war is perhaps Turner's most forceful comment on a man-made rather than a natural catastrophe, and brings to an end the sequence of large early canvases in which he continues the tradition of painting historical subjects in dark tones on a dark ground. At the same time it continues Turner's preoccupation with modern history – which he had combined with marine subject matter in a study of the Battle of Trafalgar and a large canvas, 'Spithead: Two Captured Danish Ships Entering Portsmouth Harbour' of 1808, recording the recent arrival of two ships captured at the battle of Copenhagen.

Shipwreck

1805   67⅛ × 95⅛ (170.5 × 241.5)

After 'Fishermen at Sea' of 1796, Turner regularly produced
marine subjects, which became steadily grander and stormier
over the next decade or so. In 1805 he showed this, one of the
finest of them, which was so much admired that it was shortly
afterwards engraved with great success, his first painting to be
reproduced in this way. The graphic realism of swirling water,
lurching vessels and terrified people announces Turner's intention
not merely of entertaining his audience but of convincing us that
what he tells us is the truth of nature and man's relationship to it.

The Holy Family

1803   40¼ × 55¾ (102 × 141.5)

Turner made a particular study of the great Venetian painter, Titian, during his visit to the Louvre in Paris in 1802, and exhibited this paraphrase of the master the following year. Henry Fuseli described it as 'like an embrio, or blot of a great Master of colouring'.

Snow Storm: Hannibal and his Army Crossing the Alps

1812   57½ × 93½ (146 × 237.5)

This, the culminating work in the sequence of natural cataclysms that Turner painted in the first half of his career, appeared at the Academy in 1812. It is said to have been inspired by a thunderstorm that Turner had witnessed in Yorkshire a year or two earlier; but if it relies on personal experience it transcends any local or chronological boundaries in the overwhelming vision of titanic struggle that it presents: man contends with man, and armies battle with the elements; human ambition is checked by the forces of nature. Turner may well have had a modern example in mind: Hannibal's invasion of Italy is perhaps a metaphor for the overweening career of Napoleon.

Apollo and Python

1811   57¼ × 93½ (145.5 × 237.5)

If Turner chose historical and mythological subjects to conform
to Academic expectations of serious art, he inevitably gave them
distinctly personal meanings. In this dramatic canvas, evidently
inspired by the ruggedly romantic landscapes of Salvator Rosa, he
retells the story of the sun god Apollo's defeat of the dragon
Python in terms of the bold opposition of light to darkness, good
to evil.

The Field of Waterloo

1818   58 × 94 (147.5 × 239)

Turner visited Belgium in 1817, and showed this canvas at the
Academy the following year. It is the reverse of a conventional
battle picture, deliberately using the expected broad sweep of
countryside and clutter of bodies to make a poignant and quite
unheroic point: by the light of search flares, women wander the
battlefield looking for their menfolk among the dead of both sides.
The farm buildings of Hougoumont still burn in the darkness,
and colourful uniforms glitter with ironic brightness. The horror
of war is presented as an individual and personal tragedy in a
composition of great power and theatricality.

The Deluge

1805   56¼ × 92¾ (143 × 235)

Noah's flood was a popular subject among neo-classical and romantic artists; the classic statement of the theme was Poussin's, which Turner admired (and criticised) in the Louvre in 1802. His own version, perhaps shown at his own gallery in 1805, seems to allude to the seventeenth-century master in its deliberately bold and conspicuous groups of tangled figures. The landscape itself is caught up in an apocalyptic storm of the greatest violence, through which the stable triangle of the ark is glimpsed as an unattainable haven in the midst of universal destruction.

The Fall of an Avalanche in the Grisons

1810   32½ × 47¼ (90 × 120)

A picture first shown at Turner's own gallery in 1810; he composed several lines of blank verse to assist its impact and underline the tragic implications of the event, which is not simply a grand natural spectacle but a human catastrophe:

> ... extinction follows,
> And the toil, the hope of man – o'erwhelms.

Turner may have been thinking of an avalanche which had killed twenty-five people in a cottage at Selva in Switzerland in 1808.

The ideas for many of Turner's grand subjects emerged as much from the artist's experience of nature as from his reading or study of the old masters. In about 1805 he took a house on the Thames outside London, at Isleworth, where he could meditate on the heroic past in a gentle English setting of trees and water. A sketchbook he used at the time, *Studies for Pictures; Isleworth*, contains visions of Classical seaports alternating with records of stretches of the Thames, and graphically illustrates his parallel interests and the way fresh observation fertilised his grand themes. The following year he moved to Hammersmith, and in 1807 bought a plot of land at Twickenham a little further upstream. The landscape of the Thames naturally became an important source of inspiration in these years, and he produced a series of oil studies, some apparently executed, according to the new fashion among landscape painters, out of doors and direct on to canvas or wooden panel. They are of a freshness and spontaneity that bespeak Turner's long experience of watercolour, and demonstrate his willingness to tackle any mode of expression, any technical challenge. In terms of the developments in continental landscpae painting during the rest of the century they are among his most prophetic works. Many of the finished works reflect these new interests: 'Ploughing Up Turnips, near Slough ('Windsor')', of 1809, illustrates his ability to combine a sensitive account of the realities of rural life with the subtlest evocation of misty light. It is an entirely original work which nevertheless pays homage to the atmospheric effects of a seventeenth-century Dutch artist like Aelbert Cuyp. A similarly personal reinterpretation of the Dutch tradition appears in 'Dorchester Mead, Oxfordshire', of 1810.

The influence of seventeenth-century Holland appears in another guise at this time: Turner's attention had been directed to the interior genre subjects of Ostade and Teniers by the work of the young Scottish painter David Wilkie who in 1806 showed at the Academy a scene of 'Village Politicians', to great acclaim. Turner's innate competitiveness was stirred to emulation and in 1807 he sent to the exhibition his own rustic genre piece, 'A Country Blacksmith Disputing upon the Price of Iron, and the Price Charged to the Butcher for Shoeing his Poney' – a title that seems to reprove Wilkie for the imprecision of his own, and illustrates Turner's lifelong insistence on the documentary truth of his art, particularly as it relates to the trades and pastimes of ordinary people. The same vivid realism pervades numerous lesser

A Country Blacksmith Disputing upon the Price of Iron, and the Price Charged to the Butcher for Shoeing his Poney
1807 (detail)

works of these years; rural life takes precedence over the landscape in which it is carried on; and Turner's watercolours frequently show fairgrounds and markets swarming with life and activity. There is a similar immediacy in the celebrated 'Frosty Morning' exhibited in 1813. By contrast, the large upright 'Crossing the Brook', of 1815, offers a fusion of English topographical elements with a classical framework derived from Claude. Here, with his two daughters as models, Turner reinterprets the countryside of Devon, the home of his father's family, which he had visited in 1811 and 1813, an idealised landscape almost more Italian than English.

Another grand canvas of these years is the even larger 'England: Richmond Hill, on the Prince Regent's Birthday', exhibited in 1819. A glorious summer view from one of Turner's favourite vantage-points, the top of Richmond Hill, this work brings together many of his principal interests: the bourgeois entertainments of a summer day just outside London are presented as a *fête champêtre à la* Watteau, in a landscape of Claudien expansiveness and grace.

Crossing the Brook

1815   76 × 65 (193 × 165)

In this canvas of 1815 Turner created for the first time a large Claudean landscape with a specific English reference. The view is in the valley of the Tamar on the border of Cornwall and Devon, and the silvery light of the heroic *Dido and Æneas* of the previous year is now transformed into that of an English summer day. This is a development of Richard Wilson's practice in many of his English landscape subjects. The two girls in the foreground are said to be portraits of Turner's daughters, Evelina and Georgiana.

Frosty Morning

1813   44¾ × 68¾ (113.5 × 174.5)

There is a strong element of the autobiographical in this picture:
the scene is one that Turner saw from a coach while travelling in
Yorkshire, and the coach is visible in the far distance on the
straight road to the left. The little girl who huddles for warmth in
her rabbit-skin stole is supposed to be his elder daughter Evelina,
while the patient horse in the traces of the labourer's cart is a
portrait of Turner's own 'Crop-ear'. The rendering of the thick
rime on earth and plants in the foreground is a *tour de force*, while
the starkness of the composition seems to express the numbness of
perception on a freezing winter morning.

*A Country Blacksmith Disputing upon the Price of Iron, and the
Price Charged to the Butcher for Shoeing his Poney*

1807   21⅝ × 30⅝ (55 × 78)

In 1806 the young Scottish painter David Wilkie exhibited for the
first time at the Academy: his picture, *Village Politicians*, was a
resounding success and gave new currency to the seventeenth-
century Dutch 'low-life' genre subjects which had been eclipsed
for many decades by the demand for heroic art. Turner seems to
have determined to show that he too could excel in this type of
subject, and sent his *Country Blacksmith* to the Academy in 1807.
It demonstrates his sympathy with working people, and his ability
to draw them unaffectedly as vulnerable, sometimes humourous
and always believable inhabitants of the real world.

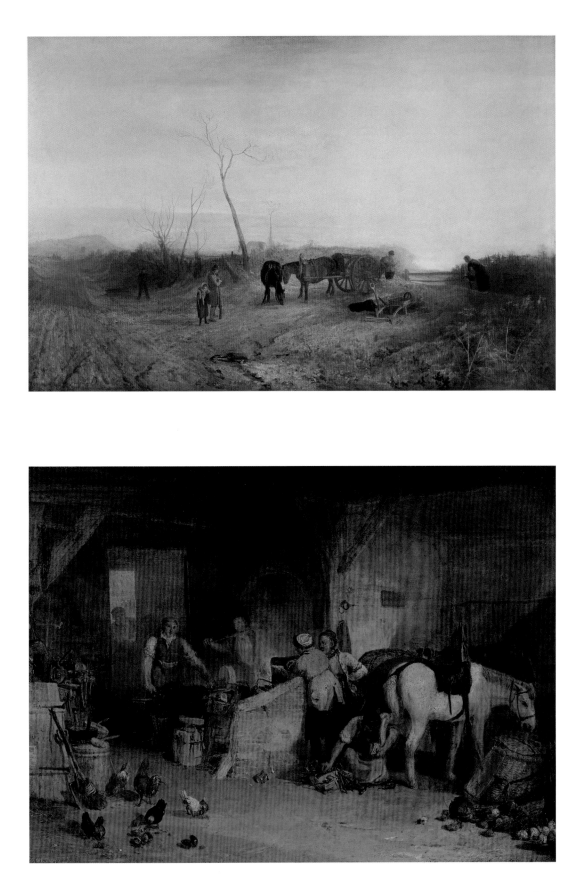

St Mawes at the Pilchard Season

1812   35⅞ × 47½ (91 × 120.5)

During the first decade of the century Turner produced a series of
views of the Thames estuary and then extended his survey around
the southern coast, having been commissioned by W.B. Cooke to
produce a series of *Picturesque Views*. This view of St. Mawes on
Falmouth Harbour, with Pendennis Castle in the distance, was
exhibited in his own Gallery in 1812. The waterside bustle shows
his keen and sympathetic interest in local activities and industries.

England: Richmond Hill, on the Prince Regent's Birthday

1819   70⅞ × 131¾ (180 × 334.5)

The sequence of English subjects on which Turner worked in the
first two decades of the century reached a climax in this large
canvas, shown at the Academy in 1819. In it the pastoral freshness
of a famous view over the Thames is united with the sweep of a
Claudean idyll and the elegant festivity of one of Watteau's *fêtes
champêtres*, which Turner convincingly evokes in varied groups of
foreground figures.

The Classical Ideal

Turner had been interested in Classical mythology since about 1805, when he had produced scenes from the stories of Venus and Adonis, Echo and Narcissus, and the origin of the Trojan war: 'The Goddess of Discord choosing the apple of contention in the garden of the Hesperides' was shown at the British Institution in 1806. He pursued these ideas in several large canvases of the 1810s. 'The Decline of the Carthaginian Empire' of 1817 is a golden sequel to the silvery 'Dido and Aeneas' of 1814, and to 'Dido Building Carthage', which Turner was later to bequeath to the National Gallery as a pendant to Claude's Embarkation of the Queen of Sheba'. The importance to him of the example of Claude, the supreme master of the ideal landscape in seventeenth-century Italy, is signalled in an even more obvious way by 'Apullia in Search of Appullus', exhibited in 1814, which is modelled closely on the Claude 'Landscape with Jacob and Laban' in Lord Egremont's collection at Petworth House in Sussex.

His first-hand experience of Italy reinforced his admiration for Claude, though by the 1820s his own Claudean style had become a distinct and powerful idiom for the discussion of ideal landscape. Many of the studies that he made in Rome in 1828 rely on a basically Claudean framework, reiterating classic patterns of great beauty, and suffused with a new refulgence of light and colour as in the beautiful study of 'Lake Nemi' with its broadly indicated masses and marvellously deft placing of a white highlight in the foreground – the ultimate reduction of Claude's ideal to a formal abstraction.

The Decline of the Carthaginian Empire
1817 (detail)

Dido and Aeneas

1814   57½ × 93⅜ (146 × 237)

Turner's first picture on a theme that was to occupy him throughout his life, this work appeared at the Academy in 1814, with a quotation from the poem that he used as his source, Virgil's *Æneid* in Dryden's translation:

> When next the sun his rising light displays,
> And gilds the world below with purple rays,
> The Queen, Æneas, and the Tyrian Court,
> Shall to the shady woods for sylvan games resort.

The light-hearted pastoral episode is treated in a full-blown Claudean manner, with a range of exquisite effects of light, especially in the distance crowded with buildings and ships, all newly revealed by recent cleaning.

The Decline of the Carthaginian Empire

1817   67 × 94 (170 × 238.5)

This canvas, exhibited in 1817, was designated in Turner's first will to hang in the National Gallery as a pair to his 'Dido building Carthage' of 1815, though he later substituted 'Sun rising through vapour' of 1807. The two Carthage subjects, then, may be read together as comments on the rise and fall of civilisation, sunrise contrasted symbolically with sunset. Turner added the following explanation to his title: 'Rome being determined on the overthrow of her hated rival, demanded from her such terms as might either force her into war or ruin her by compliance: the enervated Carthaginians, in their anxiety for peace, consented to give up even their arms and their children.' Some verses by the artist appeared in the catalogue as well:

> … At Hope's delusive smile,
> The chieftains's safety and the mother's pride,
> Were to th'insidious conqu'ror's grasp resign'd;
> While o'er the western wave th'ensanguin'd sun,
> In gathering haze a stormy signal spread,
> And set portentous.

Reclining Venus

1828   69 × 90 (175.3 × 248.9)

Besides small oil sketches, Turner painted larger canvases in
Rome in 1828, including this Venus. The goddess reclines on a
couch crowned with a laurel wreath, in the curtained alcove of a
magnificent gallery. Though unfinished, the study is an impressive
exercise in Neo-classicism. Turner probably based his figure on
Titian's 'Venus of Urbino', which he saw in the Uffizi in Florence
in 1819 and 1828, and on contemporary sculptures in Rome.
Antonio Canova's marble, 'Pauline Borghese as Venus Victrix'
could have provided a model, and perhaps this painting was
intended as a tribute to Canova, who died in 1822.

Lake Nemi

1828   23³⁄₄ × 39¹⁄₄ (60.5 × 99.5)

From a group of studies originally on a single large canvas,
apparently executed during Turner's stay in Rome in 1828. It is
a generalised sketch for the composition of a picture like, say,
'Childe Harold's Pilgrimage' (see gallery T5), but was never used
for a finished work. Indeed it seems to be an epitome of the
'abstract' classical landscape that underlies so much of Turner's
work in this vein. The highlight of blue and white in the
foreground seems to be of purely formal significance.

Italy: Landscape and Antiquity

Although Turner did not visit Italy until 1819 when he was forty-four, the art and landscape of that country had always exerted a special fascination for him. Rome, Florence and Venice were, of course, treasure-houses of art which every serious painter needed to know; in addition, for a landscape painter, the idealised Italian scenery of Claude's and Poussin's pictures had become an inescapable standard by which all landscape was judged, and by which Turner certainly judged his own work almost from the outset of his career. Long before he crossed the Alps he had produced canvases redolent of those masters; so much so that his colleague Sir Thomas Lawrence could write: 'Turner should come to Rome … He has an elegance, and often a greatness of invention, that wants a scene like this for its free expansion; whilst the subtle harmony of this atmosphere … can only be rendered, according to my belief, by the beauty of his tones … It is a fact, that the country and scenes around me, do thus impress themselves upon me; and that Turner is always associated with them …'

The influence of Claude's vision of landscape can be felt in Turner's work to the end of his life. Italy, therefore, and the ideal landscape that it inspired, takes a central place in his art, which seems to be epitomised by some of the golden Italian views of his mid-career. Accordingly, the long central room of the Clore Gallery is devoted to a survey of Turner's Italian landscapes, from the ambitious but rather overawed 'Rome from the Vatican' that he painted in 1820 immediately after his first visit, to the more generalised homage of 'Childe Harold's Pilgrimage – Italy' of 1832. The first is an elaborate tribute to Raphael, archetype of the Renaissance genius; the second an 'illustration' of the famous poem by Byron, the epitome of Romanticism.

Byron was preoccupied by the paradox of Italy's physical beauty coexistent with its cultural decline, and Turner quoted verses from 'Childe Harold' to bring out the point. A recurrent theme of several of his Italian subjects is the contrast between beauty and decay, grandeur and decline: both 'The Bay of Baiae' (1823) and 'The Golden Bough' (1834; in reserve collection) speak of the horrors of death and decay in a context of sunlit luxuriance.

One of the works that Turner exhibited in Rome during his second visit there in 1828 was the 'View of Orvieto' which he showed again in London, after some reworking, in 1830. Another picture to be retouched, and spec-

Childe Harold's Pilgrimage – Italy
1832 (detail)

tacularly, was the 'Regulus' which appeared at the British Institution's exhibition in 1837. By this date Turner had adopted the practice of working extensively on his canvases after they had been hung on the exhibition walls. His colleagues watched in amazement as he proceeded to bring a subject into being often from a practically blank white ground: it was a virtuoso performance, a *tour de force* by which, it has been suggested, Turner sought to instil some of the principles of his art into others. In practice, the exercise only contributed to the mystery that enveloped Turner's creative processes. 'Regulus' was presumably a fully articulated subject before it arrived in London from Rome; yet, for its exhibition at the British Institution, Turner seems to have reduced it to a primeval chaos of colour, out of which he set about recreating the work. 'The picture was a mass of red and yellow of all varieties. Every object was in this fiery state … The sun … was in the centre; from it were drawn – ruled – lines to mark the rays … The picture gradually became wonderfully effective. Just the effect of brilliant sunlight absorbing everything and throwing a misty haze over every object.'

Childe Harold's Pilgrimage – Italy

1832   56 × 97¾ (142 × 248)

This picture celebrates the beauty of Italy, which endures even
after the decay of the civilisation that made the country great.
The scene is imaginary – a composition of many ideal Italian
elements – and was shown at the Academy with lines from the
poem by Byron referred to in the title:

> … and now, fair Italy!
> Thou art the garden of the world.
> Even in thy desert what is like to thee?
> Thy very weeds are beautiful, thy waste
> More rich than other climes' fertility …

Rome, from the Vatican. Raffaelle, Accompanied by
La Fornarina, Preparing his Pictures for the Decoration
of the Loggia

1820   69³/₄ × 132 (177 × 335.3)

Turner's first response to his visit to Italy in 1819 was to paint this
huge canvas, the only one he finished for the Academy the
following spring. It is a complete survey of all that he had learnt
in Rome, a comprehensive panorama of the city from the
decorations of the Vatican at its heart to the mountains of the
Abruzzi which encircle it. Raphael, one of the greatest geniuses of
the Renaissance, becomes a focus for Turner's meditations on the
role of the artist in society. The objects arranged in the
foreground included sculpture, a landscape painting, a portrait
and architectural plans, perhaps alluding as much to Turner's
own creativity as to Raphael's.

Forum Romanum

1826   57³/₈ × 93 (145.7 × 236.2)

Turner planned this, the third great canvas to result from his first
visit to Italy, as a contribution to the collection of the architect Sir
John Soane. His use of a segmental arch to frame the top of the
composition may even be a deliberate echo of the segmental
ceilings in Soane's house. The dense accumulation of
architectural detail in the picture is equally a tribute to Soane's
profession and to the fantastic drawings issued by his studio to
illustrate his ideas. The subject, with its concentration on motifs
taken from the ruins of ancient Rome, complements Turner's
reflections on the high Renaissance in 'Rome from the Vatican'.

The Bay of Baiae, with Apollo and the Sibyl

1823   57¼ × 94 (145·5 × 239)

After Turner's visit to Italy in 1819 it was some years before he again tackled the kinds of ideal Mediterranean landscape at which he had excelled in the previous decade. 'The Bay of Baiae', exhibited in 1823, was his first essay of this type undertaken in the light of first-hand experience and marks a smooth and uninterrupted continuity with the earlier works in the same vein. It is as much as ever an imaginative reinterpretation of Italy; a colleague wrote on the frame when the picture was first shown 'Splendide Mendax' – 'A glorious lie'. The inherent transience of all physical beauty, however, is very much a part of Turner's picture: the Sibyl accepts Apollo's gift of as many years of life as she holds grains of sand, but without eternal youth lives on for an infinity of time, wasting away to become a disembodied voice.

View of Orvieto

1828; reworked 1830   36 × 48½ (91 × 123)

One of the pictures painted during Turner's stay in Rome in 1828, this gentle landscape approaches more closely to the topography of a particular spot than any of the others, and seems to be based on sketches made around Orvieto on the journey to Rome. It is nevertheless a highly romanticised view, and blends the Claudean ideal and the needs of topography in a characteristically poetic way unique to Turner.

Regulus

1828; reworked 1837   35¼ × 48¾ (91 × 124)

A picture painted in Rome in 1828 which Turner retouched for exhibition at the British Institution in London in 1837, this is another adaptation of the Claudean model of the Seaport. Regulus, a Roman general captured by the Carthaginians, is sent back to Rome to negotiate a treaty, which he will refuse to do. Returned to Carthage, he will be tortured by having his eyelids cut off, so that the sun blinds him. The picture as repainted in 1837 gave 'the effect of brilliant sunlight absorbing everything and throwing a misty haze over every object' as an observer described it, and seems to have been intended to present Regulus's fate in vivid actuality.

Ancient Rome; Agrippina Landing with the Ashes of Germanicus.

1839   36 × 48 (91.5 × 122)

Exhibited at the Academy in 1839 paired with a picture entitled ('Modern Rome'), this is another example of inspired architectural reconstruction – no doubt reflecting Turner's friendship with contemporary neo-classical architects. Like 'Regulus', the picture is constructed around a tragic story from antiquity, that of Germanicus Julius Caesar, father of Caligula and of Nero's mother, who died in Antioch in suspicious circumstances; his widow Agrippina brought his ashes home in an urn.

His preoccupation with colour and light is characteristic of the second half of Turner's career. The gloomy grandeur of mountains or stormy seas which had inspired his weightiest statements hitherto is replaced by the equally sublime brilliance of the sun, invading every aspect of reality and disintegrating it under our eyes. But in his journey to this final view of the world, Turner made further excursions, as a necessary corollary, into the language of chiaroscuro – the interplay of strong light with powerful shadow. In these essays he looked back, of course, to the example of Rembrandt, whose work he consciously imitated in subjects like 'Pilate Washing his Hands' of 1830. His renewed interest in interior scenes, associated as it is with these experiments with light and shade, found a channel in a series of studies of the houses of his patrons, two of which in particular yielded him inspiration of a special order.

East Cowes Castle, on the Isle of Wight, was the home of the successful architect John Nash, and here Turner was able to explore the possibilities not only of a romantic mock-castle on a bluff above the sea, but the exciting atmosphere of the Cowes regatta. His sketches of the boats leaving their moorings, or, later, beating to windward, with the castle in the distance behind them, are for pictures exhibited in 1828 (and now in other collections) which are pervaded by the sparkling summer light and exhilaration of the occasion. The sketch of an interior at East Cowes with a music party, however, is richly shadowed and Rembrandtian in its colouring, while the historical fantasy of 'Boccaccio Relating the Tale of the Bird-Cage' (also shown in 1828) transforms the reality of East Cowes Castle into a medieval dream modelled, once again, on Watteau, though this time through the intermediary influence of an admired contemporary, Thomas Stothard. It may have been in the company of Nash that he was inspired to make a series of studies on architectural themes – the canvases now known as 'A Vaulted Hall' and 'Interior at Petworth' are examples, sonorous with Rembrandtian light and shade in settings that remind us of the fantasies of Piranesi.

Petworth, in Sussex, was the other house in which Turner found an important stimulus for his work. The easy-going third Earl of Egremont was a keen collector of modern British art and host to numerous painters and sculptors, giving them facilities for working on the spot and encouraging them to take part in the multifarious life of his household. He had bought

Chichester Canal
*c.*1828 (detail)

his first picture from Turner in 1801, and in about 1827 commissioned him to paint a group of panels for the decoration of the Dining Room. Turner produced two sets of scenes at or near Petworth: one set is still at the house, the other, including the tranquil evening landscapes of 'Chichester Canal', and 'Petworth Park: Tillington Church in the Distance', was in the artist's studio at his death and now forms the centrepiece of Room T6. Petworth's old masters included many important Van Dycks, and Turner paid tribute to that artist in some of his work done at the house. An important corollary of all these pictures is the long series of studies that he made on small sheets of blue paper, in bright watercolour and bodycolour, of life in and around the house. These are still in the Turner Bequest.

While he was working with renewed interest on the theme of the interior, Turner's attitudes to what happens out of doors were broadening and deepening; his understanding of light as the medium in which everything exists and is perceived became the dominant motive of his landscape paintings, and he sought out ever more spacious scenery in which to explore the effects that most fascinated him. His later years saw the production of mountain subjects and seascapes from which many of the formal and chromatic characteristics of his earlier work seem to have been banished altogether, so that they are studies in pure light and atmosphere – the true essence of nature. Subjects that had previously been beyond the reach of any painter were opened up to him; and scenes that had been the object of other artists' attention were taken over and endowed with fresh life and meaning.

Pilate Washing his Hands

1830   36 × 48 (91.5 × 122)

Among the many artists who stimulated Turner to emulation
in the years about 1830 (when this canvas appeared at the
Academy) Rembrandt was one he had already learned much
from in his youth. It is surprising that he should have embarked
on so elaborate a pastiche as this in his maturity. He may have
been spurred on by the Rembrandtian compositions of his friend
and fellow-Academician, George Jones (1786–1869). Another
Biblical subject, 'The Burning Fiery Furnace', shown in 1832 and
also exhibited here, was executed in friendly but explicit rivalry
with Jones and again seems to imitate his manner.

Petworth Park: Tillington Church in the Distance

*c.*1828   25³⁄₈ × 57³⁄₈ (64.5 × 145.5)

The view from the south front of Petworth House across the park was one that Turner drew many times, and there are several bodycolour studies of sunsets taken from the same spot. Although this picture seems to have originally hung at Petworth it was replaced by the version there today, showing a cricket match and stags fighting. In the Turner Bequest picture the atmosphere is more tranquil, with quietly grazing deer and the figure of Lord Egremont himself striding across the turf, while his dogs rush out to greet him.

Chichester Canal

*c.*1828   25³⁄₄ × 53 (65.5 × 134.5)

Among the pictures painted for the dining room at Petworth is a view of Chichester Canal, for which this exquisite study was a preparation. It is broadly yet delicately handled, with passages resembling watercolour. Lord Egremont had a financial interest in the canal, which Turner acknowledges in his image of the ship on its glassy water; but the spirit of the picture is far removed from the world of trade or commerce: it is one of the most tranquilly serene of all his landscapes.

Music at East Cowes Castle

$c.1835 \quad 47^{3/4} \times 35^{5/8} \; (121 \times 90.5)$

One of the most celebrated images in Turner's output, this enigmatic interior peopled by figures in fancy dress has recently been found to show a room at East Cowes, and, since his hostess there, Mrs John Nash, was an accomplished pianist it is likely that it records a music party attended by the artist and perhaps shows her at the piano. Like other unfinished works of the period – it probably dates from the early 1830s – it is, however, difficult to interpret and is best appreciated as a private fantasy of the artist's.

A Ship Aground

*c.*1828   27½ × 53½ (69.8 × 135.9)

Although this canvas is the same size and shape as the series of compositions that Turner made for the dining-room at Petworth, its subject-matter is less obviously connected with Lord Egremont. It is nevertheless a very beautiful and economical evocation of the sea, perhaps designed as a pendant to the view of Brighton from the sea, for which a sketch is also in this Room. The composition was used in modified form for a finished picture exhibited in 1831, 'Fort Vimieux' (private collection).

Watteau Study by Fresnoy's Rules

1831   15¾ × 27½ (40 × 69)

In this painting, Turner pays tribute to the French artist Jean-Antoine Watteau (1684–1721), two of whose paintings can be seen in the background. One contemporary claimed Turner said that 'he had learnt more from Watteau than from any other painter'. Watteau is here deployed by Turner as a means of testing the truth of colour theories put forward by Charles Alphonse du Fresnoy. In his book, *De Arte Graphica* (as translated by William Mason) Du Fresnoy claimed:

> White, when it shines with unstain'd lustre clear
> May bear an object back or bring it near.
> Aided by black, it to the front aspires;
> That aid withdrawn, it distantly retires…

The first two lines of this verse were quoted by Turner in the Royal Academy catalogue in 1831. Turner also seems to have been pursuing this idea in the earlier picture 'Boccaccio relating the tale of the Birdcage' (1828), where the white towers of East Cowes Castle shimmer in the distance.

One place that came to have a special personal significance for Turner in the second half of his career was Venice. He had made very few views of Venice as a result of his visit there in 1819 – some beautiful wash studies and two finished watercolours are almost all we have, apart from the pencil notes that he kept in sketchbooks. But in 1833 he showed at the Academy a picture of the 'Bridge of Sighs, Ducal Palace and Custom-House, Venice: Canaletti Painting' which announced a new range of works, and the source of Turner's inspiration for them. For the next decade and a half he painted Venetian subjects of ever-increasing airiness and luminosity, which owe their origin as much to Turner's consciousness of Canaletto's achievement as they do to his response to Venice itself as a city of vast, shimmering spaces enlivened by shining water and marble, perfectly suited to his pre-occupations. These subjects were popular with his patrons, as they were with his imitators and forgers after his death; but the Bequest includes a series of fine examples, which are displayed in a room of their own. The sequence presents in microcosm the system of painting that Turner evolved, under the influence of his own watercolour technique, of rendering objects in finely applied and brilliant local colour on a white ground which shines luminously through each subject. One of the most richly detailed, with elaborately drawn architecture, is 'Venice, the Bridge of Sighs' of 1840; while 'The Sun of Venice Going to Sea' of 1843 borrows the subject, and something of the handling, of one of the numerous watercolours that he made in Venice at the time of his last visit there in 1840. As the years pass, Turner's Venice sinks ever deeper into its envelope of white mist, until buildings and inhabitants are merged into the general radiance.

Yet there persists a clear distinction between the exhibited subjects, like 'Venice, Evening, Going to the Ball', or its pendant 'Morning, Returning from the Ball, St. Martino' of 1845, and the pale, almost featureless lay-ins that survive from the studio, and which were to be worked up on the Academy's walls. There are several of these in the Turner Bequest and they have half of the room to themselves to draw attention to the important differences between what were for Turner merely beginnings and the complex, elaborate statements of his finished pictures. Although his increasing preoccupation with light and atmosphere in the last years of his career brings the two stages closer, they are nonetheless distinct. The beginnings cannot be inter-

The Dogano, San Giorgio, Citella, from the Steps of the Europa
1842 (detail)

preted in terms of this subject matter as they were never meant to be 'read' by the public. On the other hand, Turner emphasised the rich content of the exhibited pictures by giving them titles full of specific reference. His intention, even in these his most hazily atmospheric works, is still to remind us that the wonders of nature are significant only as the context in which human life is lived.

Bridge of Sighs, Ducal Palace and Custom-House, Venice: Canaletti Painting

1833   20³/₁₆ × 32⁷/₁₆ (51 × 82.5)

As with other subjects and places, Turner seems to have required the stimulus of art in order to engage fully with the reality of Venice. This, his first view in oils of the city, appeared at the Academy in 1833 just before his second visit, and so more than a decade since he had been there. It is indeed less a response to Venice itself than an act of homage to the greatest of Venice's view-painters, Canaletto. The *vedutista* appears in the left-hand corner, at work on a framed picture on an easel; the serene, resonant blue of the sky and the four-square presentation of the architectural subject indicate that Turner had Canaletto's own work very much in mind.

Venice, the Bridge of Sighs

1840   24 × 36 (61 × 91.5)

Like his Venetian view of 1833 with 'Canaletti Painting', this picture, exhibited in 1840, seems to owe something of its brilliance of colour and firmness of organisation to the eighteenth-century master, though in its assured drawing of the architecture and elaborately invented foreground groups it is typical of Turner. The atmospheric haze which gently dissolves the forms of the buildings announces the vaporous atmosphere of the Venetian views which were to follow. Some lines from Byron's *Childe Harold* appeared with the title in the Academy Catalogue,

> I stood upon a bridge, a palace and a prison
> on each hand

alluding to the Doge's palace and the prison on either side of the Bridge of Sighs.

The Dogano, San Giorgio, Citella, from the Steps of the Europa

1842   24¼ × 36½ (62 × 92.5)

This picture was exhibited at the Academy in 1842 and bought by Robert Vernon who bequeathed his collection to the National Gallery – an important impulse behind Turner's arrangements for the disposal of his own works. Vernon's picture was, indeed, the first by Turner to hang in the National Gallery. It shows the view from the steps of the artist's hotel at the mouth of the Grand Canal. The influence of Canaletto can still be felt; it was to disappear from the Venetian subjects of the following year.

The Sun of Venice Going to Sea

1843   24¼ × 36¼ (61.5 × 92)

Exhibited in 1843, this picture marks a departure from the
Canaletto-inspired Venetian pictures that Turner had painted
hitherto. It is blonder in tonality and freer in handling, being
treated almost as a watercolour, with fine strokes of bright colour
on a background almost white. A watercolour study related to the
subject exists, in the National Gallery of Scotland, Vaughan
Bequest.

Morning, Returning from the Ball, St. Martino

1845   24½ × 36½ (62 × 92.5)

A view of Venice in which the architecture and the life of the city
have become immersed in the all-enveloping mist of light and
atmosphere that pervades Turner's work of his last years. This
picture was shown at the Academy in 1845, one of a pair – the
other is 'Venice, Evening, Going to the Ball'. His last Venetian
subjects were exhibited in the following year.

Throughout his life, Turner was constantly preoccupied with the sea. From his earliest pen and ink sketches, recording his first visit to the seaside town of Margate around 1786, to the large series of evocative watercolours and oil sketches, made more than fifty years later, there was rarely a year in which he failed to demonstrate the continuing significance of marine and coastal subjects.

The importance of this type of material can, of course, be related to the island character of Great Britain, something that Turner would have confronted at the beginning and end of each of his journeys to the continent. Moreover, for Turner and his contemporaries, the idea of the nation as an island was very much to the fore during the early years of the nineteenth century, when the Channel and the shores of England represented a last frontier against the threatened Napoleonic invasion.

In his depiction of maritime scenes, Turner was chiefly indebted to the example of the Dutch school, and especially to Willem van de Velde. On one occasion he is supposed to have looked at a print by Van de Velde and muttered, 'That made me a painter'.

The Dutch influence is particularly marked in the series of pictures which Turner exhibited at the beginning of the 1830s. These include three paintings charting the heroic adventures of Admiral 'Van' Tromp (a conflation of the deeds of Maarten Harpertszoon Tromp and his son Kornelis). The canvas from this series still in the Turner Bequest, 'Van Tromp Returning after the Battle off the Dogger Bank' (1833), recalls Maarten Tromp's attack on part of the British fleet, which led to the Anglo-Dutch Sea War of 1652–4.

As in his topographical work, Turner sometimes adopted references to historic events as a means of commenting on current political developments. For example, 'The Prince of Orange, William III, Embarked from Holland and Landed at Torbay, November 4th 1688 after a Stormy Passage', represents the arrival in England of the Protestant House of Orange, but has also been seen as a comment on the long struggle leading to the passage of the Great Reform Bill in 1832, the year the picture was first exhibited.

Turner's marine subjects were not always so veiled in their allusions to contemporary life. In the famous painting, 'Slavers throwing overboard the Dead and Dying – Typhoon coming on' (1840, Museum of Fine Arts, Boston), which was once owned by John Ruskin, Turner's bloody sunset

Yatch Approaching the Coast
*c.*1835–40 (detail)

provided an enduring indictment of the slave trade from which so many great Englishmen had profited. An earlier, unfinished, canvas may depict a ship for female convicts, bound for Botany Bay, breaking up on the coast of Normandy, where the victims were callously left to die by petty-minded officials (see 'Disaster at Sea', *c.*1835)

In all these paintings, however, it is not the detail of human activity that is the principal object of Turner's interest. Rather, he addresses the much larger forces of nature: the wind, the waves and the passage of light over water. He had always been a good sailor, able to sketch in the roughest of seas, and was able to reproduce on canvas the effects he had observed so acutely. His contemporaries and more recent critics have sometimes quibbled that there are inaccuracies in his rendering of individual vessels, but his marine subjects are presented in such a powerfully direct way that the viewer is at once convinced of their overriding veracity.

In the mid 1840s, while he was still attempting unfamiliar subjects, such as the group of whaling paintings based on Thomas Beal's *The Natural History of the Sperm Whale*, Turner's focus also moved somewhat closer to home. More than thirty large canvases record his fascination with the restless sea visible from his lodgings at Margate. Inhabited by strange creatures, and characterised by storm and shipwreck, the waters that Turner depicts are at once terrifying, and are equally compelling in their austere beauty; they can perhaps be seen as the manifestation of a watery Sublime. These late works were never exhibited during the artist's lifetime, and are essentially private meditations. However, they allow us to understand something of Turner's need to give more permanent form to the awesome spectacle he found in nature.

Entrance of the Meuse: Orange-Merchant on the Bar, Going to Pieces; Brill Church bearing S.E. by S., Masensluys E. by S.

1819   69 × 97 (175.5 × 246.5)

Turner had visited Holland in 1817, and in 1818 painted his famous view of 'Dort or Dordrecht' (Yale Center for British Art) in the spirit of Cuyp. Although he still has the Dutch marine artists in mind, Turner here strips his subjects of the grandiose connotations of the old masters. The fresh open-air mood of his English subjects of the 1810s, and especially of his smaller, informal marines, is presented on a grander scale in this large canvas of 1819. Although it treats of a wreck it is not an exercise in the Sublime, rather a study of clouds over the sea, with a minor and somewhat comic incident taking place on the choppy water.

Disaster at Sea

*c.*1835   67½ × 86¾ (171.5 × 220.5)

In this, one of the most terrible of all Turner's depictions of
natural disaster, colossal waves consume a crowd of women and
children as a ship breaks up beneath them. The painting may
refer to the wreck of the *Amphitrite*, laden with female convicts
bound for Botany Bay, off Boulogne in 1833. Having run aground
in a storm, she broke up on the floodtide with great loss of life,
her captain refusing assistance as the convicts would have been
effectively freed upon landing in France. The painting does not
seem entirely finished and was perhaps too controversial to
exhibit, the wreck being subject to a protracted enquiry.

Sunrise with Sea Monsters

*c.*1845   36 × 48 (91.5 × 122)

One of the long series of studies which Turner made in his later years, exploring the effects of light on the sea, of storm and wreck, of wind, sky and water. Here his imagination runs freely on the theme of the denizens of the deep, and suggests that the ocean is peopled with sentient and passionate beings just as the earth is. At about the same date he was working on his studies of Whalers, which explore another aspect of the theme.

Whalers

1845   35⅞ × 48 (91 × 122)

Exhibited at the Academy in 1845, this was one of four pictures of episodes in the whaling industry, partly inspired by a reading of Thomas Beale's *Natural History of the Sperm-Whale*, and doubtless intended to attract the interest of Turner's patron Elhanen Bicknell, an investor in the business. Very boldly and freely handled, the picture is nevertheless given a particular documentary significance.

The New Moon; or 'I've lost my Boat, You shan't have Your Hoop'

1840   25¾ × 32 (65.5 × 81.5)

Exhibited at the Academy in 1840, this tranquil seaside study with its delicate lighting, and its humourous sympathy for the foibles of children, evokes a gentle and domestic mood far away from the storms and dramas of other late pictures.

Yacht Approaching the Coast

c.1835–40   40¼ × 56 (102 × 142)

This large study was perhaps intended to be worked up as a finished picture, and is probably datable to about 1840. It is an essay in the rendering of elemental light, yet imbued with all the strict geometry of the classical 'Regulus' (see Room T5), a firm structure of radiating lines underlying its apparent formlessness, and binding together light, air, water and the sailing ship which is impelled centrifugally as it were towards the distant shore.

The paintings of Turner's last years are animated by the same broad themes that had occupied him hitherto. The final room in the main suite is devoted to masterpieces of the decade or so preceding Turner's death in 1851, both exhibited pictures and studies. The former illustrate his continuing concern with the serious issues of human existence, while the latter pursue the fascination with effects of light and atmosphere that had governed his perception of nature all his life. The long series of atmospheric studies that he produced at this time, provide a background of generalised emotion from which the more specific subjects of the exhibited works emerge.

Those works take a remarkable variety of forms. Some of the largest and grandest, like 'The Opening of the Wallhalla' (1843), continue Turner's long-established preoccupation with crowded landscapes contrasting the role of the common man and that of the 'men of destiny' in the great historical events of Europe. In this example, the event is a contemporary one, and the verses that Turner composed to accompany it make it clear that the canvas commemorates jointly the victory of Liberty over the tyranny of Napoleon, and that of the peaceful arts over the barbarism of war. Looking back along the central gallery we are reminded of Napolean's defeat in the shadowy 'Field of Waterloo' at the far end of the vista. The contrast emphasises the often repeated theme of Turner's late years, the triumph of light over darkness, and reflects the steady progress of his own art from the sombre tonality of his early work to the luminous brilliance of his last canvases. In the 1840s Turner sometimes chose to set out such oppositions in paired works, rather than in single compositions; a similar theme to that of the 'Wallhalla' motivates the couple entitled 'Peace - Burial at Sea' and 'War. The Exile and the Rock Limpet' of 1842, where the regrets of the fallen and exiled Napoleon are set against the obsequies of an admired brother artist, Sir David Wilkie.

The square, octagonal or circular format of these paired pictures marks a culmination of Turner's fascination with the vortex, the whirling spiral of energy that defines the depth of the picture-space and binds all life and nature within it in a single dynamic movement. Perhaps the climax of the series is the pair titled 'Shade and Darkness - the Evening of the Deluge' and 'Light and Colour (Goethe's Theory) - the Morning after the Deluge - Moses Writing the Book of Genesis'. These were exhibited in 1843, and may

Norham Castle
*c.*1845–50 (detail)

Snow Storm – Steam-Boat off a Harbour's Mouth making
signals in shallow water and going by the lead

1842   36 × 48 (91.5 × 122)

The careful wording of the title should ensure that we do not
mistake this picture, exhibited in 1842, as a mere 'impression' of
wild nature. Turner is anxious to assure us that he is reporting a
specific event, minutely observed and recorded by means of his
technical mastery. The composition, based on a whirling structure
of fragmented arcs, is unusual in its freedom from the classical
models that underlie even such vividly novel works as 'Rain,
Steam and Speed'.

The Opening of the Wallhalla, 1842

Exh. 1843   44⁵/₁₆ × 79 (112.5 × 200.5)

The 'Wallhalla' had been erected by Ludwig of Bavaria above the
Danube near Regensburg as a temple in honour of the heroes of
Germany's arts and sciences. Turner showed this important
picture, painted on a large panel, at the Academy in 1843, and
two years later sent it to the Congress of European Art in
Munich. It was laughed at and returned, damaged, with £7 to
pay for its transport. The reception of the work in Europe was
ironic, for in it Turner declared his solidarity with European
culture after the barbarism of the Napoleonic Wars. It is a picture
about light, civilisation and art, a testament of Turner's ideals and
his faith in the future.

Peace – Burial at Sea

1842   34¼ × 34⅛ (87 × 86.5)

Turner's lifelong attachment to the Royal Academy and its members, and his habit of referring to other artists in his own work, come together in this commemoration of his old friend and rival David Wilkie. It was exhibited in 1842; Wilkie had died suddenly at sea the previous year on his return from the Middle East and Turner depicts his funeral off Gibraltar as a moment of profound calm. The black sails of the ship were criticised by a colleague as untrue to life. 'I only wish I had any colour to make them blacker', Turner replied.

Light and Colour (Goethe's Theory) – the Morning after the Deluge – Moses Writing the Book of Genesis

1843   31 × 31 (78.5 × 78.5)

The second of Turner's pair of pictures, shown at the Academy in 1843 and alluding to Goethe's theory of colours, which proposed that the cool and warm sides of the spectrum have their own specific emotional connotations. 'Shade and Darkness – the Evening of the Deluge' exploits a palette of blue, grey and brown while this triumphant burst of light, announcing God's Covenant with Man after the flood, is couched in a brilliant range of reds and yellows. The raised serpent in the centre of the design, alluding to the brazen serpent raised by Moses in the wilderness as a cure for plague, is a symbol of Christ's redemption of man in the New Covenant. The religious meaning of the picture is, however, complicated by Turner's verses, added to the title in the Academy catalogue. These speak of 'earth's humid bubbles', brought forth by the 'returning sun' only to burst 'ephemeral as the summer fly, Which rises, flits, expands, and dies'.

Norham Castle

*c.*1845–50   35¾ × 48 (91 × 122)

Late in life, Turner reconsidered a number of ideas which had interested him in his youth, reworking subjects from his 'Liber Studiorum' in the language of his most atmospheric oil paintings. He had first visited Norham, on the Tweed, in 1797, and had used it for watercolours and book illustrations at different periods. In this transcendent vision of morning light he reduces the image to a minimum of prismatic and shimmering colour. The drinking cow in the water reminds us that this is, nevertheless, a response to the real world and no abstraction.

Works on Paper

The interrelationship between studies and sketches in oil and the finished paintings provides invaluable insights into the working of Turner's mind, and into his creative methods. Those insights are broadened still further by the contents of the sketchbooks and other works on paper which abound in the artist's Bequest. In general, his preparations for paintings in oil were made in monochrome – pencil, pen and ink or chalk – in the sketchbooks; examples of such work are displayed in cases in the main galleries. The evolution of the finished watercolours can be followed in still greater detail, since it was not possible for a watercolour 'lay-in' to be reworked as one in oil could be. Each experimental beginning had to be commenced on a fresh sheet; and as Turner was meticulous in subjecting his elaborate compositions to careful chromatic, structural and tonal analysis he often employed many sheets in sequences of exploratory studies which lead up to a final statement. While the majority of the finished watercolours that he produced all his life were sold to collectors and are now scattered in collections public and private throughout the world, the preparatory studies for them remained for the most part in his studio. They number many hundreds and it would not be possible to display them all simultaneously; but selections of them, with other work on paper, are shown, sometimes in the context of thematic exhibitions, in the Exhibition Rooms on the second floor.

The earliest signed and dated drawings are watercolour views of Oxford and its neighbourhood. Soon after Turner had sent in his first submission to the Royal Academy, at the age of fifteen, he had begun to plan a series of topographical views for possible publication, after the fashion of the time – an ambitious scheme that was symptomatic of the energy with which he pursued his first profession. Already by 1793 he was exhibiting works that impressed contemporaries as novel and exceptionally sensitive records of light and climate, and by the time he was twenty his watercolours of cathedrals, abbeys and grand scenery marked him out as the leading exponent of the medium. Two fine finished examples in the Bequest are the 'Llanthony Abbey' and 'Valle Crucis and Dinas Bran' of 1794. His early essays in oil stimulated much technical experimentation with both watercolour and the closely related medium of bodycolour (gouache) and during the late 1790s the progress of his art was dramatic. The impact of a tour to the Welsh mountains in 1798 produced studies of a range, splendour and expressive

Shields Lighthouse
*c.*1823–5 (enlarged detail)

[93]

force unknown in landscape art hitherto; they are often very large, with corresponding depth and richness of colour. In the case of studies like the 'Welsh mountains with an army on the march' of about 1799 they adumbrate elaborate historical subjects intended to be finished in watercolour.

These developments culminated in the series of finished watercolours that he made of Swiss scenes in the years following his visit to the Continent in 1802. The Bequest contains many large chalk drawings made on the spot among the mountains, as well as a grand colour study for a view thought to be in the Pass of St Gotthard, and the finished 'Battle of Fort Rock in the Val d'Aosta', shown at the Academy in 1815 and one of Turner's most complex statements on the interaction of man and nature, in a historical context. While these Sublime subjects were occupying him, Turner was also engaged on various projects to record the buildings and scenery of England, often for private patrons, but frequently for publication as engraved plates in local histories, topographical and travel books, and, in the case of one commission, for the *Oxford Almanack*. By 1806 the range of his subject-matter in watercolour and oil seemed to merit some more widely publicised demonstration, and he began work on the long series of plates published as the *Liber Studiorum*. The monochrome designs that he made for this highly influential work provide a vital insight into his attitudes to his own art during the first half of his career. Further didactic activity of these years was his work as Professor of Perspective at the Royal Academy, for which he prepared a series of six lectures, with illustrations in the form of diagrams and large watercolour drawings. His colleague Thomas Stothard, although quite deaf, regularly attended because, he said, 'there is much to *see* at Turner's lectures'.

In the 1810s two important commissions for watercolours were in hand, the 'Views in Sussex' for John Fuller of Rosehill near Hastings, and the long sequence of 'Picturesque Views on the Southern Coast of England' for the engraver and publisher George Cooke. Although none of the finished subjects are in the Bequest, much of the preparatory work for these projects can be seen, as well as the sketchbooks used during the various tours on which Turner gathered material for them. His growing mastery of all aspects of the depiction of nature is evident in the fluent and highly personal studies in watercolour that he made on the Thames in about 1805, and in the small oil sketches that date from his tour of Devon in 1813. His first visit to Italy in

1819 gave rise to a large quantity of careful records of scenery, architecture, and works of art; and to a long series of colour studies capturing the spirit of Venice, Rome and Naples.

Of a more cerebral nature are the impressive colour studies that he made in the studio as a stage towards the production of the *Southern Coast* designs, or the series of views in the north of England for the *History of Richmondshire*, published between 1818 and 1823, and an extensive series of even more experimental trials which can be associated with the greatest of these topographical watercolour sequences, the *Picturesque Views in England and Wales*, on which Turner was working for a decade from 1825. Only one completed design for that work remains in the Bequest, the unpublished 'Merton College, Oxford' of *c*.1835–8; but the Tate's own collection also supplies a finished subject, the lovely 'Aldeburgh', which was one of the earliest to be engraved.

But several complete series of finished watercolours were retained by the artist and provide a survey of his output for the engraver during these important years of his career. The richly worked texture, with meticulous technique and brilliant colour, of his mature watercolour style can be seen in the two series of *Rivers* and *Ports of England*, which appeared between 1823 and 1828; these were engraved in mezzotint in two series which seem to have provided the impetus for him to embark on a group of mezzotint plates that he executed himself. The group, known as the 'Little Liber Studiorum', includes some of the most powerful and individual of all romantic prints; they are based on summary, but highly evocative, watercolour sketches in which Turner furnishes himself with the broadest general ideas from which to work.

By this time he was involved in yet further enterprises for the publishers, and many of his tours of the late 1820s and early 1830s were planned to supply material for new projects – the 'Annual Tours' of the Loire and the Seine which were issued in 1833–5, the illustrations to Scott, Rogers and Byron, Milton and the Bible. The 'Annual Tours' were three volumes of a never-completed series surveying the 'Great Rivers of Europe'. Turner travelled far afield collecting subjects for this. As he did at Petworth, he worked on small sheets of blue paper, using the opaque medium of gouache, or body-colour, to achieve a brilliance and intensity that seems to have been calculated as a direct challenge to his engravers. Similarly, the small-scale illustrations to the poets that he executed in pure watercolour are worked in a meticulous miniaturist's technique which enables Turner to cram a wealth of detail and immense grandeur into tiny, jewel-like designs which often embrace the same sweeping panoramic subject- matter as his larger watercolours.

The translation of his watercolour designs into engraved illustrations – whether in line or mezzotint – was of great importance to him. He supervised with a highly critical eye the successive stages of printmaking, sending back the engravers' proofs with comments and 'touchings' that reveal his penetrating sensitivity. The collections include a representative holding of the prints made after his mature designs, including a number of progress proofs. They indicate the final form which his ideas were intended to take, a form almost bafflingly far removed, in its precision of multitudinous detail rendered in black and white, from the broad colour studies with which he was accustomed to begin the process of creation.

Turner's sketching habits changed somewhat in the later part of his career. From the mid-1820s he had begun to take with him on his Continental tours a new, soft-covered sketchbook which could be rolled up in a greatcoat pocket. These 'roll' sketchbooks never entirely replaced the small notebooks in which he was accustomed to record the scenery and buildings that he encountered; but in the 1830s and 40s he increasingly made use of their more spacious pages to develop rough pencil outlines into more elaborate statements in washes of watercolour, sometimes applied on the journey, though not normally on the spot. These exist in their hundreds, and although many of them were of sufficient completeness to be sold, and have found their way into other collections, a large number remain in the Bequest. They afford a remarkable survey of Turner's activities in his sixties and seventies – as alertly receptive and as original as ever. Some are slight studies, evocative impressions of mountain villages, ravines and lakes; and there is a famous sequence of views in Venice, recording the palaces and churches along the canals, and the continual shift and shimmer of light on the lagoon. Others are more highly worked up; they achieve a wholeness that seems complete in itself. These are often drawings that Turner made as guides to his patrons when they were selecting subjects for finished watercolours; they only hint at his full intentions. The 'sample' studies of the 'Dark Rigi', for instance, or of 'Zurich', seen in a panoramic view, are magnificent tokens of his powers in old age, but must be seen in conjunction with the finished works to be fully understood. Fine examples of these, including the fully realised 'Zurich' of 1842 and the 'Lucerne: moonlight' of 1843, are to be found in the Department of Prints and Drawings of the British Museum, while grandiose late colour studies of mountains and lakes executed on a large scale exist in the corresponding Department of the Victoria and Albert Museum. Both collections contain fine works by Turner of all periods, as do the Print Rooms of the Ashmolean Museum, Oxford and the Fitzwilliam Museum, Cambridge. Among other important assemblages of Turner's work in Britain are the extensive holdings of the Whitworth Art Gallery and the City Art Gallery in Manchester, and the group of fine examples bequeathed to the National Gallery of Scotland in Edinburgh by Henry Vaughan. Vaughan also left part of his Turner collection to the National Gallery of Ireland in Dublin.

Many of Turner's greatest paintings and watercolours are scattered widely outside Britain, most notably in the United States. The National Gallery of Art in Washington, the Frick Collection in New York and the Museums of Philadelphia and Boston all possess fine examples; and the Yale Center for British Art at New Haven, Connecticut, holds the largest Turner collection outside London. The artist's output in watercolour was so extensive that there still remain numerous examples in private hands, and they frequently appear on the market. The oil paintings have nearly all reached public collections although a few are still in private ownership; they come on to the market only rarely. It is a testimony to the prodigious creativity of Turner that unknown works by him, sometimes of superb quality, occasionally come to light even today. The Clore Gallery, therefore, is far from being the only repository of Turner's work; but as the home of the Turner Bequest it is a natural centre for the study and enjoyment of his achievement as a whole.

Valle Crucis and Dinas Bran

1794–5   18¼ × 14⅞ (46.4 × 37.7)
XXVIII-R D 00703

An extensive tour of the Midland counties and part of north Wales in 1794 supplied Turner with a wealth of new subject-matter. The ruins of Valle Crucis Abbey near Llangollen in the romantic valley of the Dee were a popular theme for the picturesque topographers. Turner endows them with a new dimension of mystery and grandeur by exaggerating the height of the hill behind them, and plunging the abbey itself into a rich and vibrant shade – evidence of his rapidly growing mastery of the medium of watercolour.

The Pantheon, Oxford Street, the Morning after the Fire

1792   20 × 25 (51.6 × 64)
IX-A D 00121

By the age of seventeen, Turner had mastered the architectural topography that he had been taught by Thomas Malton, and could send this accomplished example to the Academy exhibition in 1792. It is a piece of vivid journalism, recording an event that he had witnessed earlier in the year, and combining his love of crowds and their varied interests with a perceptive study of an unusual effect of light: the early sun glows rose-pink on the icicles created by the firemen's hoses, while firemen and onlookers fill the street.

A Scene in the Welsh Mountains with an Army on the March

1799   27 × 39⅜ (68.6 × 100)
LXX-Q   D 04168

After his second visit to Snowdonia in 1799 Turner seems to have planned a pair of large watercolours on the subject of Edward I's extermination of the Welsh Bards, celebrated in Thomas Gray's famous poem 'The Bard' of 1757. An idyllically Claudean landscape, exhibited in 1800, depicts the Bard surrounded by his followers; the contrasting scene of destruction among the inimical mountains was never finished, but this large sheet was presumably a preparation for it. The vast presences of nature reduce to pigmy insignificance the long straggle of soldiers hunting their helpless prey, who watches (though unseen in this study) on a lofty crag from which, according to Gray's poem, he is shortly to precipitate himself.

The Mer de Glace, Chamonix

1802   12⅜ × 18⅜ (31.4 × 46.5)
LXXV-23   D 04615

One of the sketchbooks that Turner took with him to Switzerland in 1802 was the large book that he labelled 'St. Gotthard and Mont Blanc'. He washed its pages with a grey ground before drawing on them, and seems to have chosen subjects that would translate directly into the format of finished compositions; many of the studies were used as the bases for exhibited watercolours or oil paintings. The restricted palette of grey and ochre, amplified with scraping-out for the highlights, is well-suited to the austere landscape of the high Alps, and the book contains some of Turner's most uncompromisingly bleak evocations of mountain scenery, like this stark view of the glacier known as the Sea of Ice above the valley of Chamonix.

A Group of Trees beside the Thames

*c.*1805   10⅛ × 14½ (25.7 × 36.8)
XCV-46 D 05950

The watercolour sketches that Turner made along the Thames after his move to Isleworth in about 1804 count among the most spontaneous of his studies in the medium, reflecting as they do the new interest in naturalism that was affecting British artists at the time. But they betray Turner's innate self-awareness as a draughtsman, his requirement that every sketch should bear in it the seeds of a full-blown work. Even this relaxed and unpretentious study is carefully formulated as an abstraction in shades of black, blue and brownish-green.

Young Anglers

*c.*1809   7½ × 10⅜ (18.3 × 26.5)
CXVII-1 D 08136

The *Liber Studiorum* was designed to illustrate Turner's concern for the whole range of landscape art, from the grandest to the most informal. In the three issues that appeared during 1811 he included three plates with subjects showing children's pastimes, a theme that fascinated him all his life. This one also reflects his love of fishing, a favourite distraction from the demands of art and the Academy. It is typical of the brown wash drawings outlined in pen that he used as the models for the etched and mezzotinted plates of the series.

The Battle of Fort Rock, Val d'Aosta 1796

1815   27³/₈ × 40 (69.6 × 101.5)
LXXX-G D 04900

This complex work was shown at the Academy in 1815 with
Turner's own verses. It is a modern historical subject, and
parallels the 1812 painting of 'Hannibal Crossing the Alps' as a
moral statement of the destructive behaviour of man against man,
and the hostility of nature as barrier to man's ambitions.
Napoleon's invasion of Italy is seen as a modern version of
Hannibal's. Like a film director's eye, Turner's sweeps from
foreground group of a countrywoman tending a wounded soldier
to the distant peak of Mont Blanc, eternally indifferent to men's
sufferings.

Perspective Illustration: Pulteney Bridge, Bath

c.1810   26¹/₂ × 39⁵/₈ (67.4 × 100.6)
CXCV-114 D 17084

When Turner was appointed Professor of Perspective to the Royal
Academy in 1807 he took his duties very seriously and read widely
in the technical literature to equip himself for the writing of his
lectures. He also made numerous large diagrams and
watercolours to illustrate his remarks. Audiences who found him a
bad lecturer were glad to attend in order to see these drawings,
which often used as examples well-known buildings – Turner
even made a drawing of the interior of the Academy's exhibition
room. This large sheet shows the Palladian Pulteney Bridge, built
in Bath in 1750.

Venice: The Campanile and Doge's Palace

1819 8⅞ × 11⅜ (22.5 × 28.9)
CLXXXI-7 D 15258

One of only four watercolour studies that Turner made on his
first visit to Venice in 1819, this is the least concerned with light
and atmosphere and concentrates on the formal disposition of the
grand buildings that were to figure so prominently in his later
paintings of Venice. Indeed, with its bright blue sky and
foursquare composition, it anticipates the first of those pictures,
the homage to Canaletto that Turner was to exhibit in 1833
(see Room T7).

Whitby

c.1825 6½ × 8⅞ (15.8 × 22.5)
CCVII-J D 18143

The Turner Bequest includes two complete series of finished
watercolours for the engraver, the *Rivers* and *Ports of England*,
published as mezzotint plates in the 1820s. They are characterised
by a rich and intense use of watercolour which enables Turner to
concentrate the atmospheric range and scale of his larger works
within a very small compass. This example, from the *Ports of
England*, is a fresh and breezy marine in the tradition of Turner's
offshore subjects in oil of the early years of the century.

Shields Lighthouse

*c.*1823–5   9½ × 11⅛ (23.4 × 28.3)
CCLXIII-308 D 25431

Turner's involvement with mezzotint in the long series of plates for the *Liber Studiorum*, and later for the *Rivers* and *Ports of England* led him, in the early 1820s, to experiment with a number of original plates of his own – essays in rich chiaroscuro well suited to the velvety tonal contrasts so typical of the medium. These rare plates were never published; they are known as the 'Little Liber Studiorum'. In preparation for them, Turner made rapid watercolour studies, of which this is one.

Tours: Sunset

*c.*1826–30   5½ × 7⅜ (13.4 × 18.9)
CCLIX-101 D 24666

In the 1820s and 30s Turner was occupied with several series of views for engraving; one of the most ambitious was a project to illustrate scenes on the 'Great Rivers of Europe', and he undertook several tours in search of suitable subject-matter. The only work to be published, however, was the three-volume 'French Rivers' set, of 1833–5, covering the Loire and the Seine. The coloured studies and finished drawings for the scheme are on small sheets of blue paper, and exploit a range of vivid and intense colour. This study, brilliantly economical in its evocation of place and atmosphere, was not engraved, and its exact subject is unknown. It has been thought to show either Tours on the Loire or possibly Mainz on the Rhine.

Between Quilleboeuf and Villequier

*c.*1832 5³⁄₈ × 7¹⁄₂ (13.7 × 19.1)
CCLIX-104 D 24669

One of the finished designs for Turner's 'Wanderings by the
Seine' in the 'French Rivers' series of 1834, and an arresting
image of the contrast between sail and steam which anticipates
the theme of 'The Fighting Temeraire', exhibited in 1839
(National Gallery).

Petworth: The Red Room

?*c.*1827 5¹⁄₂ × 7¹⁄₂ (14 × 19)
CCXLIV-21 D 22683

Similar in technique and size to the 'Rivers of Europe' drawings,
the long series of coloured studies that Turner made at Petworth,
most probably in 1827 are among his most informal and delightful
works. They record with intimate warmth the great house, its
occupants and grounds, often in great detail. Here, Van Dyck's
portraits of Sir Robert and Lady Shirley are easily recognisable
on either side of the door, while the rich mouldings and rococo
pier-glass so typical of the interiors are rapidly but vividly
suggested.

A Church Spire

*c.*1828   12⅛ × 19⅛ (30.8 × 48.7)
CCLXIII-304 D 25427

The Turner Bequest contains numerous colour studies for the great series of *Picturesque Views in England and Wales* on which Turner worked for a decade from 1825. They are often summary generalisations of broad compositional effects – structures of light and colour on to which the elaborate and highly detailed content of the view would later be overlaid. They show that Turner contemplated many subjects that he never realised: this one is perhaps a sketch for a view of Grantham or Newark.

Venice: The Salute from the Calle del Ridotto; Night

*c.*1835   9⅞ × 12 (25 × 30.7)
CCCXVIII-11 D 32230

Although Turner took some time to evolve for himself a suitable language in which to express his response to Venice, once he had done so he produced a long outpouring of magical studies celebrating its soft light, its melting atmosphere and vast luminous spaces. The majority are on the white sheets of his roll sketchbooks; but one group of nocturnes uses a darker brown or buff support. A canvas of 1836, 'Juliet and her Nurse', is a view across St. Mark's Square by night, with fireworks, and it is possible that this rapid sketch was executed, from memory, at about the same date.

Edinburgh Castle: The March of the Highlanders

c.1835 $3^{3}/_{8} \times 5^{1}/_{2}$ (8.6 × 14)

N 04953

In the course of the 1820s and 30s Turner produced illustrations to the works of several contemporary poets: Samuel Rogers, Lord Byron, Thomas Campbell and Walter Scott; as well as to Milton and Bunyan. His designs were intended to be seen in the form of small line-engravings, and are themselves executed on a very small scale. His mastery of watercolour ensured that these conditions offered no obstacles to the expression of ideas as wide-ranging and imaginative as those in any of his larger drawings. The delicate yet intense miniature technique that he had perfected in the *Rivers* and *Ports of England* and other topographical series could be used with equal success to evoke sweeping landscapes within the tiny space of a small octavo page. Many of the illustrations are in vignette form; for the long series of designs he made for the works of Scott in the 1830s he employed both the vignette and full rectangular format. Here, in a drawing only 86 × 140 mm he presents a crowded scene from Scott's *Waverley* that is as atmospheric and full of life as any of his grandest conceptions.

Aldeburgh, Suffolk

c.1826 $11 \times 15^{3}/_{4}$ (27.9 × 40)

N 05236

The series of *Picturesque Views in England and Wales* on which Turner worked between 1825 and 1835 is in many ways the culmination of his achievement as a watercolourist. It covers a wide range of subject-matter, exploring the relationship between men and their environments in a host of varied settings: towns and villages, sea-coasts and harbours, markets and agricultural valleys, places of resort and places of industry. Moorland, downland, river and mountain form the background to the eternal drama of man's struggle with nature, his toil and recreation, his terrors and joys. Seas and skies, smoky mornings and golden evenings, storms and calms are all recorded with loving concern for their variety and beauty, in a pictorial language more expressive and powerful than any other evolved in the medium of watercolour. The view of Aldeburgh was one of the earliest to be completed, and was published in 1827.

Zurich: Sample Study

*c.*1841–2   9½ × 12 (24.1 × 30.4)
CCCLXIV-291   D 36147

Like Venice, the vast spaces of Switzerland inspired Turner to
new outpourings of watercolour studies in the 1840s. Some of
these he elaborated as 'samples' from which he invited patrons to
choose subjects that he could work up as finished watercolours.
This panorama of Zurich, used as the basis for one of the ten
subjects of 1842, exemplifies all Turner's love of the bustling life of
cities. He was to make a second and very similar view of the same
place in a further set of ten executed in 1845. These self-imposed
'quotas' illustrate the importance for Turner of a responsive
public, and his need to continue working within the traditional
framework of the topographical 'tour'.

Lake Lucerne: Sunset; Sample Study

?1844   9½ × 12 (24.4 × 30.3)
CCCLXIV-338   D 36197

Another of the samples that Turner prepared for his patrons in
the 1840s, affirming once again his love of the Swiss lakes and
mountains, and the infinitely variable light that defines the spaces
around and between them. These late watercolour studies
epitomise the ecstatic contemplations of the ageing artist at peace
with nature and the world.

Wycliffe, near Rokeby

image size: 7⅜ × 10¾ (18.7 × 27.3)
plate size: 11 × 17 (27.9 × 43.2)

One of the engraved plates from the series of illustrations to
Whitaker's 'History of Richmondshire' on which Turner worked
from 1816 to 1819. The engraver was John Pye, whose print of
Turner's oil painting of 'Pope's Villa' had first opened the
painter's eyes to the expressive possibilities of line engraving. The
rays of light above the Hall were not in Turner's original drawing,
and when asked why he wanted to add them Turner replied
'That is the place where Wycliffe was born and the light of the
glorious Reformation.' He was always alive to the historical and
human connotations of the places he drew and sought to reflect
them in his treatment of each subject.

The Study Room

The Study Room in the Clore Gallery is an important addition to the amenities of the Tate. London has already two well-established Print Rooms, at the British Museum and the Victorian and Albert Museum; these both contain, among much else, large collections of works on paper by British artists. The Tate Gallery has acquired drawings and watercolours of the British School only incidentally to its principal task of representing paintings, but over the years has accumulated a fine group ranging from the early eighteenth century to the late nineteenth. Its main strength lies in its holdings of watercolours, which include most of the major practitioners in the medium from Paul Sandby to the Pre-Raphaelites. Nearly all the romantic landscapists of distinction can be found here: Thomas Girtin is represented by the work which is perhaps his masterpiece, 'The White House, Chelsea', and there are examples by De Wint and Cox, the Varleys, Crome and Cotman, Cozens, Stothard, Linnell and Palmer, Bonington and Boys, Callow, Lear and Muller. Of the Victorians Ford Madox Brown, Rossetti, Burne-Jones, Millais, Ruskin and Charles Keene are to be studied in drawings of many different types. The centrepiece of the collection is the outstanding group of works by William Blake, one of the most important in the world, which complements the Turner collection as a comprehensive representation of one of Turner's greatest contemporaries. Constable is also present as a draughtsman, and his collaboration with the mezzotinter David Lucas is recorded in a complete set of the published plates of the *English Landscape Scenery*.

When these works have been displayed in the main galleries of the Tate they have necessarily been seen under restricted lighting. Now that the facilities of a Study Room are available, they can be viewed in the most favourable conditions, with access to works of reference and suitable space for note-taking and research. This does not mean that drawings, watercolours and prints will cease to be displayed in the galleries; but those not on view will be more accessible than they have been in the past. Visitors are welcome to use the Study Room by appointment. University teachers who wish to bring groups of students for seminar purposes should also make appointments, stating precisely which material they require to use. This will be prepared for them before the arrival of their party, for which an area of the Study Room will be set aside.

Visitors to the Study Room are requested to deposit all bags in the cloakroom on the ground floor, and to ensure that their hands are clean (a washbasin is provided at the entrance to the Study Room). They should make known to the staff the titles and reference numbers of works they wish to see; these can be ascertained from the catalogue cards and reference books on the open shelves. A form is provided for applications for individual works, and staff will help visitors find the correct registration or catalogue number for purposes of identification. Items requested are brought to the tables, where pencils only are permitted to be used. Sketchbooks by Turner are not normally accessible to students, since they are for the most part extremely fragile. A representative selection of the sketchbooks is on show in the main galleries, and a photographic archive will, it is hoped, supply any information needed, while obviating unnecessary handling. In addition, a microfilm of the Turner Bequest is available.

The purpose of the Study Room is to enable all who are interested in drawings and prints to examine them at leisure in pleasant, quiet surroundings without the inconvenience of controlled lighting or glazing. Drawings are generally mounted in sturdy board mounts which permit handling, although these too should be treated with care. They are stored in solander boxes, which are kept horizontally, and drawings should always be stacked in their boxes when they are not being examined. It is important to avoid touching the surface of a work of art, either with one's hands or with the edge of another mount. When a work is being looked at it should lie flat on the table, or be placed on one of the stands provided; in no case should any work be placed on top of another, except in the solander box. Books of prints are similarly available to visitors on request, and they too should be handled with the greatest care. They should not be placed on stands, but examined flat on the surface of the table.

It is the duty of the Study Room staff to ensure that all items are treated properly, but equally they are there to give assistance, and members of the public are encouraged to ask for guidance. Scholars and art-historians will, of course, avail themselves of the new amenity; but it is hoped that many people other than specialists will take advantage of the opportunity to enjoy the intimate and often very personal works of art that the Study Room contains.